6/18

CONTENTS

A WILD RIDE

Imagine a snowboarder coasting down a mountain. The wind changes direction, and suddenly she's going up the mountain! How can she do that? She's holding a large kite. The power of the wind and the kite help pull her along.

RISK FACTOR

Snowkites are much bigger than the kites you might fly in your yard. The bigger size gives them more power!

SNOWKITING

By Hal Garrison

Gareth Stevens
PUBLISHING

Please visit our website, www.garethstevens.com. For a free color catalog of all our high-quality books, call toll free 1-800-542-2595 or fax 1-877-542-2596.

Cataloging-in-Publication Data

Names: Garrison, Hal.
Title: Snowkiting / Hal Garrison.
Description: New York : Gareth Stevens Publishing, 2018. | Series: Daredevil sports | Includes index.
Identifiers: LCCN ISBN 9781538211212 (pbk.) | ISBN 9781538211236 (library bound) | ISBN 9781538211229 (6 pack)
Subjects: LCSH: Kite surfing--Juvenile literature.
Classification: LCC GV840.K49 G37 2018 | DDC 797.3--dc23

Published in 2018 by
Gareth Stevens Publishing
111 East 14th Street, Suite 349
New York, NY 10003

Copyright © 2018 Gareth Stevens Publishing

Designer: Bethany Perl
Editor: Kate Mikoley

Photo credits: Cover, p. 1, 29 Timofeev Sergey/Shutterstock.com; pp. 1-32 ver0nicka/ Shutterstock.com; pp. 5, 7, 11, 17 Norbert Eisele-Hein/LOOK-foto/Getty Images; p. 9 Wallenrock/Shutterstock.com; p. 12 simonovstas/Shutterstock.com; p. 13 Scott Dickerson/Aurora/Getty Images; p. 14 Anton Kudelin/Shutterstock.com; p. 15 ericlefrancais/Shutterstock.com; pp. 19, 23 Parilov/Shutterstock.com; p. 21 NORBERT MILLAUER/AFP/Getty Images; p. 25 Andrei Gilbert/Shutterstock.com; p. 27 legenda/Shutterstock.com.

Printed in the United States of America

CPSIA compliance information: Batch #CW18GS: For further information contact Gareth Stevens, New York, New York at 1-800-542-2595.

SNOWBOARD

Some people might think snowboarding and skiing are enough of a **thrill**, but snowkiters want even more adventure. They use a snowboard or skis, as well as the extra force of the wind, to sail across the snow and into the air.

RISK FACTOR

People who snowkite on skis often choose shorter and lighter skis than those used for regular skiing. This lets them catch more air!

SKIS

WATER OR SNOW

Snowkiting is kind of like kiteboarding. Kiteboarding is a sport where people use large kites to move across the water on a board sort of like a **surfboard**. Instead of moving on water, snowkiters use the wind to help them move on snow and ice.

KITEBOARDING

RISK FACTOR

Some people think snowkiting is easier to learn than kiteboarding because it's easier to balance on snow than on water.

THE RIGHT KITE

One of the most important things a snowkiter needs is a kite! There are different kinds of kites. They come in many sizes. Smaller ones work best when there's a lot of wind, while larger kites can help when it's not very windy.

RISK FACTOR

The kind of kite used in snowkiting is called a power kite. Most are shaped sort of like a rectangle, but with curved ends. Some are **inflatable**.

The bigger a kite is, the harder it is to use. This is because more **material** creates a stronger force. A smaller person might have a hard time controlling a large kite. A larger person needs a bigger kite to pull them around.

RISK FACTOR

When there's enough wind, snowkiters often fly dozens of feet up in the air!

IN FLIGHT

When they're in the air, snowkites are often curved and look like a C shape. Many have 4 lines, or strings. The wind presses against the kite and pulls the person holding onto the lines across the snow or ice.

RISK FACTOR

Snowkiters can reach speeds of up to 70 miles (113 km) per hour!

STAY IN CONTROL

Snowkiters control the kite by holding onto handles or a bar that is joined to the lines on the kite. Many snowkiters also wear a **harness** to make it easier to hang on, especially in strong winds!

RISK FACTOR

Moving the bar or handles a certain way can take power away from some kinds of kites and let the snowkiter control the ride.

BAR

HARNESS

17

THE BREEZE

There's one thing needed to snowkite that's just as important as the kite itself—the wind! Without any wind, the kite's not going anywhere. The best conditions for snowkiting are those with steady wind. Unsteady or sudden winds can be hard to snowkite in.

RISK FACTOR

Some snowkiters prefer faster or slower winds, but many say winds of 12 to 25 miles (19 to 40 km) per hour are ideal.

DANGER IN THE WIND

Snowkiting is a fun sport, but it can also be dangerous. The wind can change directions and quickly move a snowkiter somewhere they don't want to be. That's why they need to make sure the area is clear of **obstacles** and not near any roads.

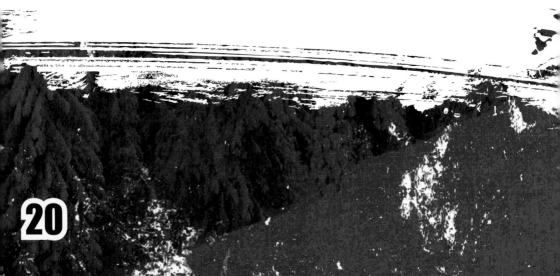

RISK FACTOR

Flat land is much safer to snowkite on than mountains, and it can be just as fun!

Wind conditions can be hard to guess. One moment, a person could be sailing through the snow perfectly fine. However, a sudden, strong wind might blow the person up in the air, with little control over where they'll land.

RISK FACTOR

Sharp rocks and pointy pieces of ice are sometimes hidden under the snow and can be a danger to snowkiters.

THE COMPETITION

Some people just enjoy snowkiting for fun, but others **compete** in the sport. Some events are judged on how fast the snowkiters go. In other events, the winner is the person with the best jumps and coolest moves!

RISK FACTOR

Skiers and snowboarders are often judged separately in snowkiting competitions.

LEARNING THE SPORT

Some snowkiters started off as regular snowboarders or skiers. Others were kiteboarders first and wanted to enjoy a form of their sport in the winter. People new to snowkiting should take lessons and learn from a skilled snowkiter.

RISK FACTOR

Even longtime snowkiters shouldn't go out alone. Staying with a group is safer.

CATCHING AIR

Snowkiting's not suited for just anyone—it takes a daredevil! This sport requires a lot of practice and at times might be scary. Skilled snowkiters sometimes travel hundreds of feet through the air before landing back on the snow!

RISK FACTOR

Many snowkiters keep in shape for their sport by lifting weights in a gym.

SAFETY TIPS

ALL SNOWKITERS SHOULD:

- start by using the smallest kite that will carry their weight.

- be able to safely control their kite.

- take lessons and learn from a skilled snowkiter.

- make sure the area is clear of dangerous obstacles and not near a road.

- go snowkiting with other people.

- wear proper safety gear, including a helmet.